THE GOODBYES

JOHN ASH

THE GOODBYES

CARCANET NEW PRESS / MANCHESTER

To
IAN ROBINSON

Acknowledgements are due to the editors of *PN Review, Ambit, The Shearsman, London Magazine, Palantir,* and *Kudos* in which some of these poems first appeared; and also to the Radio 3 'Poetry Now' programme.

First published in 1982 by
Carcanet New Press Limited
330 Corn Exchange Buildings
Manchester M4 3BG

British Library Cataloguing in Publication Data
Ash, John
The Goodbyes
I. Title
821'.914   PR6051.S/

SBN 85635 452 X

The Publisher ackmowledges the financial support
of the Arts Council of Great Britain.

Printed in England by Short Run Press Limited, Exeter

CONTENTS

PART ONE

'All the voluntary movements are possible—crawling through flues and old sewers, sauntering past shop-fronts, tip-toeing through quicksand and mined areas, running through derelict factories and across empty plains, jumping over brooks, diving into pools or swimming along between banks of roses, pulling at manholes or pushing at revolving doors, clinging to rotten balustrades, sucking at straws or wounds; all the modes of transport, letters, oxcarts, canoes, hansom cabs, trains, trolleys, cars, aeroplanes, balloons are available, but any sense of direction, any knowledge of where on earth one has come from or where on earth one is going to is completely absent.'   W. H. Auden

The pianist commences the sonata about the angels and
    the rain.
It is so slow, so lingering we will soon be fast asleep

dreaming of pink rooms filled with musical animals and
    roses
while our teeth rot in sympathy, and outside
the autumn air grows dense as a preserving oil.

We must start now on the long route back
to 'the evidence of our senses' but it is hard,—
we **may** have to unlearn as much as we learn,

besides, we distrust all the approved maps and signposts . . .
So the threat arises of a sojourn as long as a life
in some commonplace purgatory
of cacophonous motels and braided intersections. Yet
these are not all that modern life has to offer us
and the town is not a monster to be run away from,
screaming into headlights and blank night: thus, escape
from one dilemma only lands us in the swamp
of another, and the smell is worse than ever . . .

We could invoke tradition, speed up the film of the flower
or imitate the procedures of music, in the hope
that these evasions might lead us, by way of doors
casually thrown open as if nothing were at risk

back to the dim point of departure. But how
can this appear as it was? It is only a confusion
of inclined planes, corridors and theatre boxes,—

a fake painting called 'Melancholy Of The Set-Square'.

This too is a question
of perspectives tapering into nothing—
disposal-chutes, elevator-shafts: a dream
from which we are excluded—

a city: factories like cathedrals,
palatial crematoria, avenues
lined with trees that might have been
drawn from failing memory
in a windowless room. Of course,
the shadows are ominous and still,
the warehouses empty and burglar-proof,
the windows vast and dreaming . . .

Something collapses in the old film studio:
the dust falls back exactly into place,
filling the outline of a pressed flower or a book,

and the trains arrive and depart unnoticed,
leaving thin wisps of smoke like commas
dissolving on a white sky:

the words are missing.

INCIDENTAL MUSIC

for Malcolm Scott

The musicians are writing letters of complaint.
They can't sleep, it keeps snowing in their hotel bedrooms.

Their instruments wait, tarnished in corridors,
for the polisher to come. Their shoes have left them

and winter follows them from Berlin
to Adelaide. During Schoenberg

the conductor mistakes a celesta
for a flexitone, and the sweat
from his tossed hair blinds the violas.

In Hong Kong one doesn't want to play Brahms
or talk to the ambassador's wife;

in New York one would prefer
to play a Symphony of Seven Stars
not pastorals for sheep . . .

There is general concern about
the anal fixation of the first trombone,
political agitation among the oboes
and drug abuse in the first violins—

rhythms drown in undifferentiated foam
and the new concerto from Sweden is
the equivalent in sound of wrapping paper and wet sand.

This isn't living. No,—
a museum should not be carried
on the backs of men,

and the musicians are writing letters of complaint
the musicians can't sleep

the musicians comb snow from their hair
the musicians refuse to play on the raft
the musicians are weeping the musicians are drunk—

with regret they have buried their instruments
in hope of better times.

An indestructible debris of plastics
burnt rubbers crushed metal

piled to the horizon's long drone

and above it in the isolation of a saint
a boy plays over and over
the chord beyond which his hand will not stretch.

                    *

The bombs have fallen
harmless as walnut shells
into the middle of the bathing party.

                    *

Strange, the customs here—

girls are buried with their boots on
and lockets round their necks
containing photographs of last year's boyfriends.

Note also the importance
of vehicles, water and musical instruments.

                    *

After the inspiring visit
of the semiologist
the citizens decided it was time to do something
about the crisis,—I mean the terrible boredom
everyone was feeling about then
even though the sky continued brilliant
and blue like the sky over Sounion.
It had gone too far;
it was getting into everything—
diluting the iced beers, corroding chrome bumpers,

swarming like a crowd bearing very dull placards
into any unattended space and refusing to budge
once established. Things were bad. No wonder
the kids had taken to satanism
and the worship of obscure fetishes . . .

*

Billy came home with his head shaved and a mark
in the hollow of his cheek that would not scrub out
even with a stiff shaving brush. He was to die soon
in a country his terrified mother couldn't even imagine
as she stifled him with emotion, driving him out—
though this was the last thing she wanted to do—
on to the streets of the boring town where the drive-in
sold dildoes with onions, driving him into
the muscular arms of his charming friend Pete
who had admired, insincerely, the bleary water-colours
in which her son's gaunt face was constantly dissolving
into a landscape of unformed but very sweet desires.

*

On scrubby hillsides
chalets and villas glimmer faintly,
ringing with cocktails . . .

The swimming pools are suspended
in mid-air
above the dry river bed.

The dead girl's uncovered face
stares up towards
the electric fences of her father's rose garden

and a chorus of young people stumbles away
through blue boulders,
retching, without an exit line

and still bored.

14

Doris is about to enter a convent.
She remembers the happy times
she spent in the log cabin with Bill.

Ada has recovered the use of her limbs.
Unfortunately, during the wedding
a child is suffocated by a bouquet
carelessly tossed into its cot.

Hubert's mother has been kidnapped again.
Perhaps Doris will change her mind
at the last moment? Agatha, of course, hopes not . . .

to the memory of Erik Satie

What are the people like there? How do they live? . . . I'll admit I've never been there, but that won't stop me telling you all about it.

The people there weep often, alone in rooms with candles and old books. In their terrible Augusts they make black entries in their diaries. Their songs are doleful but the dances at funerals can be very lively,—danced to the rhythm of whips, gourds and snares—and the colour of mourning is ochre. . . . They are fervently religious yet their government is atheist: to discourage worship the roofs have been removed from all their churches. But any government is provisional. Each summer, and sometimes during bad winters there are riots in the streets of their windswept and lacustrine capital. There are so many informers, however, that the police always know in advance the exact time and place. Thus everything is done properly: vendors may set up their stalls, street musicians choose their stands, and respectable families gather in perfect safety to watch the instructive spectacle. . . . Tobacco and sheep are the basis of the economy. Out of patriotic duty everyone there chain smokes at incredible speed: they regard the medical reports with furious disdain, and their ceilings are stained a deep, yellowish-brown (like papyrus scrolls from the cemeteries of Fayyum). Their sheep are, without question, the shaggiest and most unkempt in the world,—each animal a mobile continent colonised by vast tribes of ticks. . . . They are always washing things in water so soapy it is barely fluid, and yet nothing ever seems clean. And they think of themselves as Hellenes! Arbiters! . . . In their typical symphonic music a huge, squelching adagio like a sea-slug is followed by epileptic dances, catastrophic marches,—the whole concluding in a welter of chromatic swoons. Their orchestras are very large. They play everything *fortissimo*. (And—horrors!—they re-orchestrate Mozart!) Their national

16

anthem is an arrangement of the mastodon-trumpet theme from Scriabin's 'Poem of Ecstasy'. (When the massed bands of the Republic begin to play this it is difficult to persuade them to stop. . . .) And yet, strange to relate, they possess singing voices of an exceptional and haunting beauty. . . . Their buildings are either hen-coops or Piranesi dungeons, Nissen huts or Sammarran mausoleums. . . . Their poets write constantly of their failed marriages, failing health, unhappy childhoods and—for variety—the apostrophes to stars of laundresses and cabmen. . . . It rains often, yet the vegetation is sparse in many areas and the summers can be oppressively hot. Steam rises in great clouds from their low roofs, and from the many balconies where drenched furs are hung to dry. Steam rises and moisture drips ceaselessly onto their unsurfaced streets in which a score of jeeps and hay-carts have their wheels stuck fast. Their flags hang always at half mast. As if ashamed their rivers vanish underground. . . . In the south of the country there are extensive lakes of warm, grey mud. . . . The train there moves in fantastic, slow loops,—a baroque embroidery expressing an infinite reluctance to arrive. They think, with good reason, that the world is forgetting them. . . . They greet each dawn with a chorus of deafening expectorations.

X: and end, marked on each window and the central door.
No florid and coloratura voice, or last phrase of a waltz.
Its grandeur, an emptiness now made literal, the astonished
trees find their roots in air and sicken over a new abyss in
which their shadows are confused, feeling for the sundial
out of reach.

The sentiment is questionable: regret for a vanished order
which, if it still existed, we'd dream of destroying like any
nation of the colonised.

OUR LIVES: A SYMPHONY

1. Allegro ma non troppo

And these people have great wealth.
We should greet them in a fitting manner.
They have travelled here in coaches of a new design.
They are surrounded by indestructible glass.
They are like the most valuable exhibit in the museum,—
the gold mask, the only surviving fresco
from a tradition of three centuries. And they have seen
nothing to rival this. The evidence

of our poverty and great bitterness is
a new pleasure to them: the oaths thrown at them,
the stones are an entertainment,—
explosions of colour, savage music, dance-mania
you might expect to find in some obscure recess
of Empire, but not here at the centre
in ports from which the viceroys departed. . . .

The parade crumbles,
and when an empty car goes up in flames
it is so surprising
it seems to be happening in slow motion:
it is still going on. . . .

2. Adagio (lamentoso)

You have to pass under
so many derelict arches,—

viaducts, aqueducts

to reach the eastern rim
of the city
from which the transports leave

19

at increasingly infrequent intervals.
Not many wish to visit
and someone, one supposes, has to stay

since the buildings still stand
against the sky, solid and vacant

as cemetery statues. Our lives
have been folded away like a letter

bearing a message of terrible
urgency
and never posted.

3. Scherzo and trio

We love our city.
If we do not who will?

We have the biggest shopping-mall in Europe
and the biggest dispensing chemist

also the biggest hospital
the biggest mad-house, the biggest prison

the largest number of empty churches
and blocked canals (this—
of course—is the undiscovered Venice
the covert Petersburg
that Alexandria the sea snatched away. . . .)

more beer is brewed here than in any other major city
and a blue mist envelops the tall buildings

the Japanese tourists
on the escalators ascend like saints, smiling
at magnificent blooms of smoke above the inner-suburbs.

4. Molto moderato (quasi passacaglia)

and the young couple emerge
from the hospital, its long facade
stretching for what seems a mile in either direction
of windows, windows. . . . She
has one thin hand hooked over his arm (it
might be an empty glove) and she is carrying
a child wrapped in a plaid rug.

They descend the steps
and the town descends further before them,—
an infinite declension, darker and darker. . . .
each ledge or street burdened with long ropes
of motionless people waiting
transport. The lights fail
briefly in a thousand windows
and resume, weakened. A woman

rounds a corner pushing a handcart before her,
and it is filled with dolls: small corpses,
each in a different, bright Victorian costume:
scarlet, mauve, yellow. . . .

These are for sale, and a man shows
interest. He bends over them
and it must be that every vein in his face
has broken: engorged,

the nose pendulous, he fingers the synthetic
hair, and asks the price. On waking it is

the *price* dominates recollection,
its black and white stays fixed

like the first mountain you ever saw
or the first blood, the first death. Listening

into the night, you hear
a hammering, the nails sinking in as windows
are blinded, and it still

goes on, even as sleep returns,
at no great distance,—

a wooden tapping (coffin lids)
a hammering. . . .

'How like a headlamp
is the moon,' he raved, 'the headlamp
of a patrol-car. And I know
it is useless to resist. . . .

My civilisation has ended,
and I liked it so much: people were kind to animals
and, every weekend, remembered to take
to aged parents, bunches of pink and pale blue flowers;
all houses were *cottages* or *villas*,
and somehow had an air of looking
happily out to sea, even when there was no sea,—
yes, in those days the whole world resembled the environs
of Winchelsea and Rye. . . . But now it is ended,
and *someone* must be to blame, some American, I should
    think . . .'

But his words began to blur
like a cartoon run at double speed, like
the passing continent with the brief sparks of its sleepless
    towns,
and the wind was in my throat, blocking reply;
it was as if all the old problems of friction and inertia had
    been solved,
and we were moving imperceptibly over prairies of mirror-
    glass towards
the destination from which nothing could swerve,—
a city in ruins and newly rebuilt,
a place of contorted glass and vertical, white metal
forcing its slatted piers and opulent roof-gardens out
into an ocean for ever flashing with superb malice . . .

and here the antique machines
of judgement and division have rusted

into a harmless dust, colouring, a little, the sunset,
and each new arrival experiences
a feeling like love or sexual attraction, but also
unlike and new, accompanied by a dazzling calm.

It was not an intellectual face,—
white, with the mute look of a rose about to be doused
with a powerful insecticide,
and she never understood why, in her presence
perfectly sensible men would lose all control. What
was it she *did?* It cannot
have been anything she said. . . .

Further incidents: she borrowed the old earl's Rolls
to take her to the station, and stole
his breakfast kipper to eat on the train;
the whole family had a wonderful time that summer
in the Tuscan palace lent by an infatuated count
except that all the floors were so highly polished
that, by the end of their stay, sprained wrists and broken
    ankles
were scattered through their ranks like floral tributes
at the end of a charity matinée;
she was horrified when her younger brother's hair
was cut short, declaring it 'an atrocity',—
and never forgot this. . . .

Everything worried her, even the great rose-window of the
    cathedral,—
but there was always the consolation of 'the dear country-
    side',
rolling away like vellum or old velvet into a distance where,
unquestionably, something very nasty and probably foreign
    was
continually going on,—a kind of dust storm, an old argument
the wind wouldn't let drop, which she wasn't about to lend
    an ear to.

In 1917 Regie wrote to her: 'You remember Roughton?
Joined the Balloon Corps. Poor chap. Shot down

last week at 6,000 feet. He landed not far from me,—
shockingly foreshortened, but still recognisable by his
   cigarette case.'

The man she eventually married was a hopeless drunk.
She hardly seemed to notice. Despite this,
and his rumoured womanising, the marriage 'worked'.
During her second war she kept goats—'such
useful animals'—and wrote to the ministry advising
the placing of giant magnets in the parks of the capital
to attract the German bombs there,—
'thus sparing many lives and many fine old buildings'.

Like her beauty, her myopia was legendary:
often she would sail past acquaintances of several years—
quite unawares, leaving a fine foam of grievances glittering
   in her wake.
In her extreme old age she still posed for photographs
wearing a large hat trimmed with brilliant blue ostrich
   feathers
(and this is a form of courage ought not to be disdained),—
her autobiography (ghost-written)
might have been called 'A Milliner's Chronicle', or
'The Philosophy of Hats',—recording, as it did,
the different phases of the horrible century she lived in
in terms of face-veils, lace-work, birds' wings, pins, and fake
   collapsing flowers:
a method not without advantages. As good as any, you might
   say. . . .

Everywhere he saw his own image,—
his perfect face. . . .

When he rode out of the city, the people
gathered to admire him: a ribbon
of faces, fixed on this one face
and haunted by its indifference. They said:
'as beautiful as a painting,' and we
feel a chill cast across the years
for we know there is another painting
that does not hang in any gallery;
there is a film that will never be shown:
by a rear door the assassin enters
carrying a mutilated head.

The passion he inspired cut him off
in a distance where his horse's hooves
sent up jets of red dust. His protector died:
reading the obituaries, unmoved,
he thought it was not his death until
the admiring crowd became an avenue
of statues leading to a grave

prepared in advance. A silence
like a long drum-roll
allowed no final act of grace.

POOR BOY: PORTRAIT OF A PAINTING

Difficult to say what all of this is all about.
Being young. Or simply arrogance, lack of patience—

a misunderstanding about what the word maturity
can mean when exchanged among 'real' adults. . . .

I don't know what kind of plant that is, but it
is green and has a small red flower

and the glass it strives towards is latticed,
yellowish and cracked. Beyond it

roofs are bunched together like boats
in a popular harbour
and through it the inevitable light falls. . . .

And the light is art! It is arranged *so*,
over the bed and the pale dead boy,
his astonishing red hair, the shirt rumpled like sculpture,

the breeches. . . . The breeches are a problem:
no one can decide whether they are blue
or mauve. Versions differ. But the light

is faultless. It can hit anything
whatever the distance,—
for example, the squashed triangle of white lining
to the stiff, mulberry coloured dressing-gown,
the torn-up sheets of poems or pornography,
the oriental blade of pallor above
the boy's large, left eye-lid or even the small, brown
dope bottle lying on the scrubbed floor
almost at the bottom of the picture. Of course

much depends on the angle. Much remains
obscure, but this only enhances
these significant islands of brilliance,

exposed and absolutely
vulnerable to our interpretation:

there is nowhere he can hide the hand that rests
just above his stomach as if he still felt horribly ill.

'Few realised it, but the aim was to be
completely impersonal and modern
like office furniture or a display
of automatic washing-machines. . . .'

Cut flowers scattered over the chairs . . .
a familiar voice, so familiar it may be yours,
saying 'these long nights still
aching towards dawn like a burnt throat. . . .'
The search for the place and the formula has begun again, in
    earnest,
but paradox and elision rule our every gesture in that
    direction
(accustom yourself to this confusion,—
it is your climate: the music too loud, the lights
blinding or stygian, the hour
too late) . . . and even when speech is
nearly redundant,—as may be the case at this moment—
we like to retain certain clichés, for the sake
of their beautiful transparency (like that of over-exposed
    slides)
or, to put it another way,—they hang on
like that compromised personality you disowned years ago....
Thus: the exclusive concern with 'loving' and 'possession'
is terrible; in the end, people have no other reality,—
they are shut away for life inside this small frame that allows
no graceful or surprising movement. And it is
a kind of *movement* we want above all else. But there is
    conflict:
everyone wants to claim some section of the graph,—
some colour or pitch, a curve out of the frame. . . . This
is a comedy, I suppose, but there's the problem of distin-
    guishing between the players,—
names, faces, numbers . . . flicked out of existence
like charged particles; new instruments of calibration are
    needed.

I acknowledge their failure,—
the lives all purple prose and no plot
but this can't stop me feeling something like 'love' for these
     dead people.
I worry about their photographs, fading so fast the whole
assembly could soon be reduced to a single raised eyebrow,
and the letters from numberless, magnificent hotels in The
     South
are getting badly smudged (it could be tears). . . . But this
is a study I will return to often, opening the blue book of
     years,—
hearing the wine bottles and crockery breaking in the depths
of a Mediterranean night scrawled in haste on a postcard....
There must be something that will outlive us
in so much despondency and elation, causeless or
caused by so many things, there isn't the page could hold
     the catalogue,—
and why not admit it? it is best to live simply,
according to conventions, safe from random metamorphoses
or sudden accesses of memory (the morning
light falling on the crumpled party dresses, the grapefruit
     segments . . .)

Now, ideas of flight and falling
become involved with drumbeats and shadows:
the saxophone extrudes
a long slick of hair oil from the nineteen-thirties
and the violins scream like 'Society Women' jumping from
     the hotel in flames! . . .
Your world has ended . . . *again*. . . . And that smile
so carefully judged to deflect all criticism
is the true sign that you are lost like the idea of a just
     society . . .
or would be were it not possible for you to
turn away. . . . And whether all of this appears as hell or
     heaven
depends finally on your angle of approach,—
the axe you are grinding, or not as the case may be. For

31

it should be possible to assemble once again
the *idea*, the memory so brutally dismembered
on the hard ledges of this night gleaming in descent under
the downpour, between the sheer walls of decayed ware-
   houses . . .
and a new voice calmly interposes like lavender
between layers of fine, folded cloth stored away
as used to be done for the sake of young inheritors
whose gratitude or ingratitude cannot alter the marvellous
grace and tenderness of the original gesture;
and it is all inlaid with a nostalgia that somehow seems to
   come
from a point far in the future,—

'I cannot remember the name, yet I know
it was a place of continual springtime
filled with ornate, metal buildings and the windings of a
   river,

and anyone who went there fell immediately in love
and began to paint the picture of their love
in vivid colours which might be only the rails of a balcony,
the edge of a table, a drawn blind, a bowl of peaches, some
   cigarettes
whose brand name concealed a message of such moment
the whole world hung on it without knowing.

I cannot remember the location (the maps
were redrawn a long time ago) yet I know . . .'

the idea was to be . . .
was (only) to live in hope.

PART TWO

'Into that world of freedom without anxiety, sincerity without loss of vigour, feeling that loosens rather than ties the tongue we are not, we reiterate, so blinded by presumption to our proper status and interest as to expect or even wish at any time to enter, far less to dwell there.'   W. H. Auden

The bed had a person in it.
The sun was climbing through warm mist.

It had been raining, now it was snowing.
The book on the table was wrapped in a bright flag of
    convenience.
Two small girls, dressed in blue and red nightgowns
were arranging the cards in the shape of a fat man
who seemed to be signalling desperately,—

'Over here! Over here! . . . You know me,
you surely must remember; we met on Thursday,—
O, it was a day of unforced amity! the sky
was veined like a slice of marble or blue cheese;
you told me to give up my job in the bank and spend more
    time in the greenhouse,—
also, I was to eat less and read more. . . .'

Twigs snapped in the fire. The fault opened like a sigh
and the whole suburb swayed gently south,
dislodging from the breasts of several matrons, pearls
that rolled under the wheels of speeding cars. Suddenly

everything was tired and wanted to go to bed.
We did, and you. Also they. And it.

Curtains began to blow. Birds were standing
very watchful and still, in the heaped snow. The scene
shuddered like shoulders
when the sneeze can no longer be suppressed:

general embarrassment—a rosey blush—
consumed the features of the day,

which is to say, it was now evening
where it had been morning.

'O sole, true Something—This! . . .' S. T. Coleridge

With vague attributes, they all wander in here
at one time or another. Often
I wish they would stay longer, if not to speak,
then perhaps to take on some more certain form,—

a swirl of colour (orange or green) in an otherwise
transparent marble that has just emerged,
of its own volition, from years of exile under the sofa.
And why has it come to us at this moment?

The unimpressive apparition might mean something,—
for an unexpected pause in the recitation of a letter
can have more power to disturb than a whole succession
of subsiding Valhallas, and we can barely read the words

announcing the discovery of the lost girl,
the mystery of the mésalliance. Is it the dim light?
Or tears of the sort that are compared to pearls? . . .

We care about this more than a little
but will never know: this evening's visitor comes as an odour
of freshly baked bread that follows me
down the narrow corridor from the little bedroom lined
    with books,
and there is nowhere it can come from! It seems
friendly enough, 'concerned' even. A response from the air.

Or something that has stepped outside of me for a moment
to 'take the air' like a fluttering heroine after the execution
of some especially fevered nocturne, in search of refreshment
to stretch its limbs a little, and to remind me that I have been

Neglecting it. And I *have* been neglecting it. This is obvious,
for it most resembles a guest at a crowded party whom you
    have introduced to no one:
a charming guest but with a look of reproach.

I have forgotten so many things and this is one
and wants to take its place among the salvaged,—
among flowers from the fifties or the colours of a paintbox,
under the brim of a hat, beside a gold river at the heart of
    an old province
that is growing with each intake of breath
as the fresh odour spreads, claiming the most impervious
    objects,
reviving the colours that had begun
to fade to white scarves of the death of this place
that is now big as a democracy, vivid as a nettle's sting,—
and we cry out, hurt! The task ahead
is momentous but pleasurable: you have to invent, or—
which may be the same thing—remember
the language of this place, its peculiar history, cuisine and
    carnivals;
what people did in its eighteenth century; whether it is
appropriate to talk of 'serfdom' after the close of its
    nineteenth century,
the ambiguous relationship of this to the rise of a
    bourgeoisie. . . .
And so on. You might also prepare new
and superbly accurate editions of dissonant masterpieces
by its early church composers, or discover
in a foxhole, the last act, lost for decades, of its most
    famous opera.
When you have done all this, conducted a census
and completed the catalogue of native birds, you will be able
to find the place where, in the midst of this much folded and
pleated landscape   the loaf rises like a monument:

now free from hunger and confinement,
we inhabit its shadow.

Perambulant flowers, snow-
sculptures, soap dishes:
the hostess blames them for her sleeplessness;
the dinner guests cover their ears.
They go on singing, poor birds,
in the middle of the lake and
are not understood. Each auditor

resembles the aborigine first
confronted by
a serenade from Salzburg,—
the movements passing swiftly far
above, like blurred constellations,—
beautiful in their blue way but
referring to different myths,
ones he couldn't sing:

*'You do not understand
the profound love we feel for one another
and for you. And this
is the principle of our society, its
glittering podium: our colour signifies
our selflessness, our wings close over
the young we are denied and at nightfall
we are possessed in terror by the foreknowledge
of our deaths. But this too will be given
if it is demanded by you—*

*you grounded at some distance, on
terraces, in houses, in the light.'*

And the cry goes up from the table:
'Enough! Pass the red beans, the rough wine.'

In my father's house there are many rooms,
some of them too beautiful to speak of—
three dining-rooms for example, and every surface
polished. Also a conservatory with parrots,—
real parrots. And beyond the countless
windows, the Great Pool on which the allegorical
statues float by: the one representing *Sleep*
is my favourite, I think, but it is the tears of *Hope*

have filled the pool. In my father's house are many
flowers and a gold piano. But why
has the book of poems by Maeterlinck been torn
in apparent fury? The children have been
sent to bed in the middle of the afternoon.
A full glass of milk stands by every bedside
as monitor and guide. There are whispers and sighs.

Now it is raining and a flock of blue birds
lets fall the quilt. The embroidered
message tells me—
sob! that I don't love you any more.

But I do, and the feather pillow bursts. *Achoo*.

THE THRESHOLD MOMENT

with acknowledgements to the Chic Organisation

The continual, gnawing dissatisfaction of people patrolling
   a basement
looking into each others faces and finding nothing
was glossed by the music. 'Rebels! . . . Rebels! . . .' The
   refrain
nearly finished us. But now, in time for you to breathe, the
   entertainment collapses,—
a coloured tent, the poles protruding all ways, the cloth
   drenched. And here,
sprouting carnivorous flowers of mould, are volumes one
   to the infinite
of the world's saddest and most boring stories, sagas of
   perpetual disappointment,—
the right one always eluding, a kind of Cinderella syndrome
with an enormous surplus of princes and ugly sisters. . . .

Speak to the owl, if you can find one. The jig is up. Our
   ideas have left us,—
they were at the bottom of the glass. And something opens
   to a great depth,
like the blue of the sky when birds are lost in the severe
   alps of commerce.
A kind of regressive feeling sets in, like an ache. Time to go
   home.
Only . . . a certain, over-reaching ambition remains,—

to go further, refusing to accept this as the end point,
   signalled by old, deafening clocks,
leaving the chaste houses of parents and professors far
   behind,
as a thin mirage drawn on the air by sombre children good
   at sums;

to be lost from sight, shameless monomaniacs, recognising
   only what we touch—

what touches us—the small tremor in which the world
    consents to be extinguished
as a pot of flowers (geraniums perhaps) is extinguished
when it falls from the sill of a high tenement window:
    something
remains, but nothing you'd recognise. But you exaggerate
    (and *why not?*)
you are thinking of Italy or some other place of light, and
    floral tributes
where the legend is: 'These people really know how to live.'

You may take pleasure in feeling lost, but, of course, you
    remember
how quickly we can traverse the long way back, knowing
all the brambles and wires by rote,—knowing too well
those ravines like lying smiles of welcome that would
    swallow us, until
we arrive at the place where the new day romantically
    extends
its pale and still cold hand with an old-fashioned courtesy
    like lace. . . .

And it is a promontory where trees have rooted in the stacks
of an abandoned library now barely distinguishable from
    the space around it,
and a staircase leads down from the dust of the central door
towards the distant city, which naturally only *seems* distant:
it is almost in your hand,—a kind of cubist garden wherein
a crowd of people move at blurring speed, under foliage of
    smoke,
among pillars built with mirrors, reflecting vast sunsets.

Or it is only the memory rising from some such name
as Ctesiphon, or the chessboard of Ch'ang-an, Tu Fu
    lamented. . . .
But no, it is real, you insist, and the musty names I drag up
    depress you.
Look, the ocean is receding from the streets and squares

and those who have slept awake! It is another legend,
    another fable,
one that ends happily. And each individual—
their clothes, their hair or the small movements of their
    hands,
impresses us as the element of a pattern we wouldn't, just
    now, alter a stitch,
although we know sadness is in it like an ink-stain. The
    conquest

has been accomplished, and no one was subjugated. I am,
    you are
eager for the oncoming night,—its lights, its advertisements,
    the sound of its cars. . . .
The sky looks like storm clouds: each of us conducts
    lightning.

Site chosen, permission granted (sir!), materials assembled,—

a few, neat, round clouds cast decorative shadows; people and perspectives arrange themselves around the space the building will occupy; the landscape resembles a quilt with a design of willows, small lakes, striped, tame animals in flocks. . . .

Blue-prints? There are no blue-prints. . . .
(And, no, those aren't building-blocks;
They're cubes of rock-salt brought from a mine,
So big it contains a church.)

Church? Library? Concert-hall with cafés and exhibition space? The question of function will be decided when the work is complete. And the work is all *air, punctures, truancy:* lace-making in three dimensions with a time-span of centuries in mind.

Yes, it is hard work, and those who would prefer to *carry horses* should get on with that.

Now it is time for the community singing, and here are the sandwiches for the work-men,—some salami, and some egg mayonnaise. This goes on for a year or so with bursts of activity and long, pleasant pauses: the 'pauses' are just as important as the 'activity'. How could the work be completed without them, or the songs?

—Songs of the Uzbeks, songs of the Azerbaijani, the Bosporani. . . . Their harmonies are visible in the rising superstructure. But rhythm came first: it goes down into the rock.

At last it seems to be finished, and applause breaks at the sight of this static spectacle that goes on and on to the crazed eye of an oval sky-light. A space for paradox: if we made casts of the coffers in the ceiling they would resemble Mexican pyramids. . . .

There is so much to enliven the eye,—to lead it on like an excited child deeper into the fairground. But of course this isn't a fairground—not even the one in Petrushka—it more resembles an intoxicated perspective drawing by some Platonic idealist of the High Renaissance. So many balconies, staircases, octagons, windows of various shapes, rotundas, superfluous numbers of alcoves in which whole cities seem to be present,—

Vienna, Petersburg, dead Miletus, Anuradhapura and proud Tigranocerta. . . .

And these are no longer centres of government, military operation or bureaucracy. They exist solely to be enjoyed, —places of rose-bushes, vines and lawless amusements, gentle and barbarous towns! . . . And if the original concept is unrecognisably distorted in bearded cornices, fluid door-frames, unsprung arches, inverted spandrels *it doesn't matter:* the architect—a dwarf Walloon—is soon appeased.

And people seem to find the building useful somehow:

the café in the water-gardens on the roof is doing very good business (thank you) and a band plays most Wednesdays and Fridays, and everyone doubles on saxophone, and,—

The lead-singer is so handsome
She hardly needs to wear
A gardenia, but does: it is an act of homage,
A token of nostalgia
(The only one permitted here). At night
The flag-poles and radio-spires
Are flood-lit from the bottom of a lake.

If the wasp is stuck in the wet disk of blue
in the open paint-box we won't be able to paint
our breathtaking adventures on the horizon,—

the place the bird-calls come from: their truth would be in
      doubt,—
also it seems a discourtesy not to know the names
of these singers whose cries are like coloured flares, burning
on a wide circumference by which we judge direction
and scope. But now, the blistered sills are hot
and we're listening and leaning into a distance that's
immense, capable of any transformation—

How far? How deep? Who will come with us?
Everything is in there, even the mountain
where the elephants go to die. Sad, the elephant songs
in the morning. We'll come back with their bones
and with them build huts in the water-meadows:
we'll live on marigolds, on marigolds. Ivory will keep us. . . .

Now the ballet's about to begin. The signs are hung
at a friendly distance and the dew dries on them.
The clear air's full of the feeling of curtains rising
and everyone's ears are tuning up. The woods
are wrapped in a new colour, unmentioned in the shade-card
and the statues are hidden beyond nettle-patches. Their
fallen hands have been carried off finger by finger
by field mice and buried: they always looked ill. . . .

When the bell strikes we pull in our heads
and the world composes itself like a deep pool
around the angel from Italy, the chrome flowers in the vase,—

we're kneeling in a room but we're somewhere else
there's a ceremony but the pauses
and orations are measured behind our shut lids

we're found we're lost we're sinking we're rising
like bubbles from fish-mouths like feathers on a breeze
in so many depths of blue turning to violet—

and it begins

like a song like a stomach ache like a sleep
like a haze of heat. How far? How deep?

If the river falls over a cliff that is high enough
it will never reach the ground: it will end
in rainbows a hundred feet up.

Despite or *because of* all the wrong notes,
the desired effect was in the end achieved:
that of an aura surrounding a body of great naturalness and
    beauty,—

almost as if a plan of the heavens were expressed to us
in terms of the crudest riffs and reels played on the upright
    piano,
without in any way diminishing a sense of vastness and
    brilliance
quite beyond our ordinary apprehension (the dishes,
the bus-timetables, the steamed spinach)

—a 'courtly dance' for which the feet have not been found,
in which, as it turns out, the most archaic-seeming phrases
were written down in a rush, *only yesterday*,
when the troubadour unclasped his quartz watch. . . .

And it was in the evening when the rainstorm suddenly
    approached
across the random divisions of a remote and densely-peopled
landscape in full leaf. Afterwards there were pools

on window-sills, and the humble diversion of mopping
    these up
only served to enhance the great sense of clarity and
    purpose that was forming in the room.

The final shape of things was strict,
of a Vitruvian severity, but this allowed a freedom
which otherwise might not have been risked, and the result
was a rhapsody in which tall figures, untouched
by our anxieties, were not embarrassed
to appear.

PART THREE

La vie entière est en jeu
Constamment
Nous passons à coté du vide élegamment
sans tomber
Mais parfois quelque chose en nous fait tout trembler
Et le monde n'existe plus

Pierre Reverdy

NO MAD EXQUISITE

for John Lenton and John Ashbery

ıe said, 'the half of it is nothing'. At once
the objects began to multiply and all had
an attractive transparency about them, like names
written in water: the bowl of apples,
the brochures with romantic illustrations of cheap hotels,
the empty bottles. . . . Swept away
they were immediately missed as though
they were the only things in the world
worth knowing and keeping: the saving remnant, sludge of
    gems. . . .
She said 'all regrets are idle, that is their charm'
and there were arias next concerning
our personal loneliness in cities too large and too much
the same to be understood. And bloody spears
decorated with what looked like canary feathers
or syringa petals were offered as subjects of analysis,—
works of a 'lost' tribe. It was all getting too much.
Why did we feel so *guilty?* And then the face on the vase
    began to speak,—

'I am the wounded composer's
dead child, and these are tears—
damn it, not baubles or bangles
though you can hang them from your ears
at interesting angles.
The opera was in arrears—
that's why I died. . . .'
                        A huge wasp
has taken up the road, syphoning the pumps.
We won't go that way, we always
feared them. . . . Besides
he seems to be saying we could have sex right here
in this window and no one would see us
except perhaps some insect-figure perched on the water
    tower

49

or the pointed folly (an obelisk) or the chimney
leaning Pisa-fashion over the defunct mine. . . . Hey!
you can't go in there. Put down that air-rifle!
And what were you shooting at? I can only see
some big leaves and, under them, some possibly lethal
    canisters
of no special importance (this was a dump, you see,
from the last war, or the one before that,—
the one where they found a new, white flower like jasmine
twined round the wire barriers). But 'No'
he said 'although
I am yet young I know more than you
who haven't looked across this torrent, even though
you know the bridge and walk here often
looking for the firewood you no longer need in the tower
I can see behind you on the hill that always travels with you—
I mean the tower that has always haunted me,
dominating the mesh of these outlying towns cast forget-
    fully over a desert,
from a time long before I saw it or you. No,
I was firing into an *abyss*, watching as the birds died
in their thousands, and all this for the sake of their music.
You see, I don't want to be like The Others, whoever they
    are. . . .'

And so (suddenly feeling myself part of the story) in turn I
    said,—
'Well, if that's all there is to worry about, you and me
could go to sleep right here, curled together beside this old
    highway to Bombay or Manchester,
though, come to think of it, it *does* look like rain. . . .
But these leathery leaves will serve for protection. Here,
    take one.'

To which the desperate reply came singing,—
'You don't know about the poisons.
You can't smoke here, or drink, or eat: the sign says so. . . .'

There was something in this: the sky seemed to be
coming down like machinery in a prison scene.
It may just have been night coming on
with a puritan gesture, but we weren't taking any chances.

The report still had to be made.
It was vital to the safety of water and trade.

We grasped firmly the shears
which cancelled our fears.

Soon the wool would fall from our eyes, and then what ore
would cover, in heaps, the granite floor!

A Venetian palazzo, a Roman temple, a French chateau, a dome from a mosque in North Africa. . . . Cast-iron capitals in the form of lotus flowers, gable-ends, dormer windows (after Mansard), chimneys like vases,—the solid memory of smoke. . . . Continent of geometric forms gleaming darkly after the rain inhabited by democratic communities of birds . . . ô ville que l'on dit industrielle . . . here are the green canals of childhood. . . .

You are approaching a news-stand, and you look up. And there, flooded in a sunlight denied to the street's depths, balconies curve outwards, pilasters taper or swell towards leaves encased in scrolls . . . a Titan blows a conch and windows break upwards through the architrave that should limit them. . . . The dictionary of architecture lies open, in three dimensions.

(In the city our idea of 'the country' is conditioned by camera angles and peasant costumes in dull productions of Chekhov: even allowing for our ignorance, it cannot be *so* interesting. . . .)

Also there are places where shadowy columns rise towards inscriptions in dead languages, and they are like film-sets waiting for the ultimate crowd scene,—the entry into Rome or Thebes, the banquet at Persepolis—which now can never be filmed. Alas! the producers have gone into tax-exile. . . . So the space remains unoccupied but for the slow accumulation, in colourless layers, of puzzled speculation concerning forbears who required such a gulf between a dim, blue ceiling and the conduct of their business.

Crowds. Collisions. Dusty parks. Red tulips
Abstract street-battles. Muted, sexual outcry.

Sometimes it is as if the whole of life were lived in the sub-basement of a department store, among packing-cases and

52

forgotten typewriters. The buildings stand imbued with sadness. The last firework has exploded in the night-sky of summer and the children know that tomorrow the work begins, the confinement. . . .

Patrons, captains and pay-masters! The city would like you to appreciate its recent attempts at efficiency and self-criticism,—its severe new face of yellow brick. Like a convert to an unforgiving faith it divests itself: the old statues and ropes of stone flowers are pounded into a dust that clogs the ventilation systems of its half-empty hotels. . . .

place où ma vanité devait se pavaner . . . I can neither forgive nor forget any of this.

1   Again, the weather's wrecked the picnic.
All those drenched frocks,
tomato slices in flooded bowls—

so English! the clouds, the downpour
as evasive terms
for a continuing epic of bad faith
and commonplace ill-feeling. . . .

2   Yes, something *has* changed
irreversibly. It speaks out of silence
like a radio announcer
off-cue. Time to remove the varnish? Yes. . . .

3   All departures cancelled:
the pillars in the painting are grey
and the sails of fishing boats
drawn in with no hope of unfurling,—
blue cranes of the container-depot
motionless. Only the immense
sandstone cathedral looks as if it might move—
gliding off, a gothic liner, leaving
the city burning behind it. . . .

4   Dun cows like stalled cars
are dumped in all the streams:
someone has *smoked* the landscape.

5   The glass graph-paper of office buildings catches
no sun this evening, and this expresses
everything we feel about the situation and do not
    understand,—

How could you love a person like him or like her?
They are ignorant,—they think *all* Italians are Catholic.
Their blond hair gets into everything, even sleep. . . .'

6   With things as they are it's difficult not
to feel like a newly arrived exile
even though you've lived here for years.
Principal cities are renamed and history
slides into a dull dream of foreknowledge
in which past mistakes are cancelled.
Who are these heroes appearing in the false guise
of youth? these avatars of
expediency? No one is convinced. Even
the sky is discoloured
like the pages of a novel left open at a window,—
the plot so mechanical every word or sigh
fell with a thud to rot slowly where it fell,

staining the carpet at the place
where the corpse is marked in chalk.

7   And the clouds! The clouds!
O, a thousand sobbing goodbyes!

Overweight and weeping bitterly
they are dragged off to interrogation:

they confess everything,
including your address. . . .

8   A fog is expected,—
the first 'real pea-souper' in years.
'You can't rely on the weather. . . .'
Everyone agrees on this
while the window darkens
like someone's mother's brow in splendid
anger: 'Child! O
ingrate! My lichen! Little cuckoo, go
into the world: it is
a narrow corridor and we do not know its end,—

unless it be this blurred picture
of a river or a tree, branching in Africa. . . .'

9   Voices rise in confusion,—
     counterpoint of amateurs. Talk
     turns to the furniture of permanence.
     Contracts are signed, houses change hands
     (hands change houses) but yours
     is not (is never) the face seen at the window
     advertising with a cold smile
     its new contentment. That smile! You'd think
     death were abolished, and people
     not starving with infinite slowness—
     là-bas, là-bas: their hands make a thorn-bush
     on which your morning paper is impaled.

10   Friend, you'd better board up that window,
     never know what might go down to-night—

     an ice factory is planned for your garden
     a steel mill for your living room
     a six-lane highway for the hall
     and even now, directly beneath your feet
     huge coal-seams are being explored. . . .

     The walls are shaking. The light
     is drunk. Goodbye.

11   This is only goodbye—

     a handkerchief like a white wing
     a tear in a bottle, a moist hand
     encountered in a hotel foyer,

     the goodbye of silence,
     late music and exhausted nerves

     goodbye stretched to the furthest point
     of perspective, where
     the small spaces of our lives
     submit to immensity—

the grass that continues as an unbroken blue undulation
over mountain ranges and stepped cities of moss

the goodbye of calls
crossed and misdirected
like the preparatory sketch
for the beast in a fable,—

bearded with sharp ears
the face a kind of mesh that shines towards us
as the goodbye
of everything we are uncertain of

the goodbye that leaves you ruined
(split cast for a bronze figure of defeat)

the goodbye of goodbyes
it wants no more—

the goodbye of words
that rub themselves out

the goodbye like a blank stair-
case leading
back into whatever you were.

FERNS AND THE NIGHT

'Und wir hörten sie noch von ferne
Trotzig singen im Wald.'

This is the sort of place you might arrive at after a long
   journey
involving the deaths of several famous monsters,
only to be disappointed almost to the point of grief.

Heavy clouds hang in a clump above a wide, perfectly level
   plain
which is the image of a blank mind. Night is falling.
There is a wooden house, a lighted porch: it is a scene of
   'marvellous simplicity'.—
too marvellous perhaps: the very grain of the wood offers
   itself
for our admiration, and the light has such 'warmth'
it is hard to restrain tears. The clouds are now distinctly
   purple,
agitated,—a kind of frantically stirred borsch, suitable
   backdrop
for some new opera's Prelude of Foreboding, but not for
   this ambiguous scene
of severity tempered by domestic tenderness, in which we
   find
the 'young mother' looking for her child. . . . He has run off
into deep woods nearby, leaving his blue train crashed on
   the lawn.
She calls his name, but after the third call it becomes diffi-
   cult or exotic music,
a series in retrograde inversion, an entry in the catalogue
   of unknown birds:
she is already elsewhere, her torch illuminating the pure,
chlorophyll-green ferns of a forest, and the torch itself, a
   flame. . . .

She finds that her bare feet are wet and that she is looking
   into a puddle,
Seeing the clouds reflected and her face (the moon also).

She calls again
but has forgotten where she is, or whose name she is calling.
Her own perhaps?
The wooden house, the lighted porch seem unreachable,—
artfully lit, a glassed-in exhibit in some future museum of
the human.
Ferns and the night conceal the child whose laughter
distantly reaches her.

'Ain't it a shame
Can't give it a name
The moment you do
It flees from you.'
Ashford & Simpson: from the LP *Is It Still Good To Ya*

It is all happening inside a globe, a kind of
rosarium: the problem of age, the problems of the Age,—
this circling like bored fish. And that is all.

We see that you are dissatisfied,—
that we are, and, on a certain level of granular
iteration, always will be: the sand
is inside our shirts and our shoes, and the sandwiches
will have to be abandoned on the cold,
rubbish-strewn beach. In shelters against
the rising wind the fan-vaulting looks pretty
but leaks, and the petition never reached those
probably mythical persons-who-matter,—

we see it floating for ever downwards
in the bottomless stairwell of some vast, bureaucratic
    chateau. . . .
So allowances have been made
and the soft house-lights of sympathy trained on the matter,
almost as if a party of orphans were present,
and yet. . . .
                Neither stoic nor operatic
there is a dampness about these goodbyes which really
too avidly anticipate the catastrophe,
and your despair is a luxury produced at too great a cost
in basements where the smoke and steam are solid:
the doors don't close as your fear imagined they would
in that hotel at the end of the world,—softly,
one after another, a scale on a piano stuffed with felt.

Something escapes,—
something holds its colours, still sings. . . .

O *sanglots et soupirs*
like village spires around the face
misting over in The Icon Of All The Childhoods,

it is not you! but it is
changing and unalterable,—

the steps and gestures of a very old ballet
only half-remembered and recorded in a colourful, obscure
    notation
first made flesh before unheeding audiences in wigs and
    bankers' suits
that now appears, having no further need to impress,
as branching arms asking 'Why?'—an absolute
simplicity—against a white cloud (burnt at the edges
by a light that has travelled further than imagination)
resembling that flower whose misadventures have more
    than once
startled you with tears, innocent and unexpected as snow
    in summer.

Or that is how it sometimes seems to be,
often in the wake of great music.
It may be different for you and should be,—
all definitions approximate and free. . . .

Call it a river,—

call it a summer or an open house:
a mild rain is falling through sunlight onto benches
shrubs and a fountain,—characters
in this story that is not a story. Strangers
are welcome here, and you have finally walked out
of that mean and dusty apartment you once called
a self. The air tastes good, doesn't it?
And you won't need your books or records with you
since, now, you can recall them all at will—
the words, the notes will no longer seem like props
but will be free structures in which you can loiter, or not
as the mood takes you. Similarly,
you will like the people here but if you choose
to ignore them no offence will be taken. A lake
is nearby, unseen, but altering the light falling across your
    knees
and, like an unjust tax, the accent of regret is abolished.

But see . . . the fountain doesn't work any more
and the strict plan, though admirable, can't
be imitated: it is just one of many things
that elude us or are 'gone for ever', like rosewater down a
    sink. . . .

Yesterday's a spectre in classical dust sheets.
Today's a lad dressed with ragged insouciance.
And a new quality of attention is needed: silences
have to be orchestrated, portraits drawn with invisible ink
if we are to know what is really taking place
beyond this pale surface that is so satisfying in itself. . . .
Some minor romantic heroine may be dying
in a bare, panelled room no one ever visits, or
perhaps a child has lost his way in the blue woodlands of an
    illustrated book

and now the brambles come alive to bind his ankles,—
or it may be that some buried hope, that once seemed
    foolish,
is about to issue forth to demand immediate
construction of the forms it can live in: now it is *the only
    rational solution* . . .
a loggia by Brunelleschi, a portico by Inigo Jones
in which the evening light of a summer, not far from the
    Aegean
has been permanently installed.

Meanwhile the sun has risen again,
like a chord in C, through bars of cloud;
and everyone is still looking into that garden
or walking in some other garden or park
exchanging words about
the flower bed in the shape of a clock-face,—

and it really tells the time—
our time, in generous periods like Schubert.